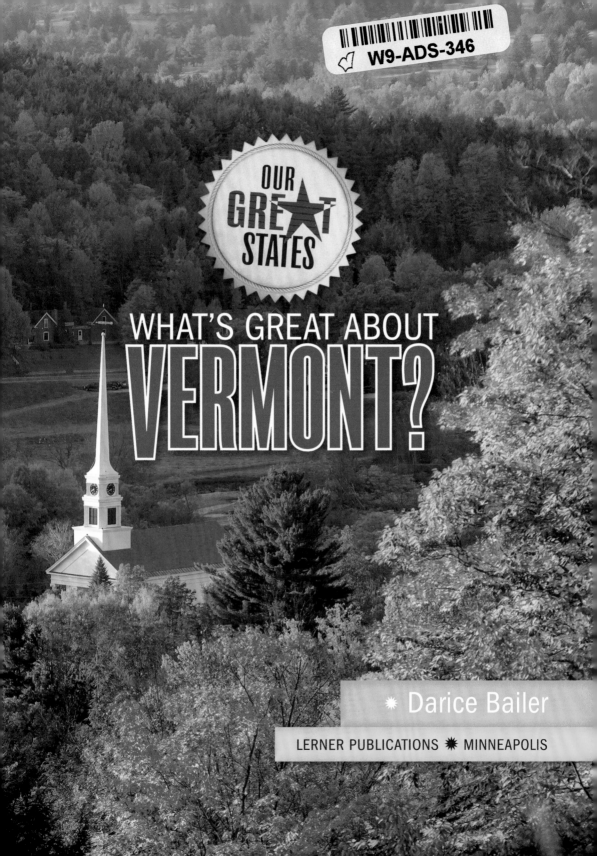

OUR
GRE★T
STATES

WHAT'S GREAT ABOUT
VERMONT?

✴ Darice Bailer

LERNER PUBLICATIONS ✴ MINNEAPOLIS

CONTENTS

VERMONT WELCOMES YOU! ✳ 4

CIRCUS SMIRKUS ✳ 6

BRATTLEBORO ✳ 8

REVOLUTIONARY WAR SITES ✳ 10

VERMONT MAPLE FESTIVAL ✳ 12

BILLINGS FARM & MUSEUM ✳ 14

Copyright © 2016
by Lerner Publishing Group, Inc.

Content Consultant: Douglas Slaybaugh,
Professor of History, Saint Michael's College,
Colchester, Vermont

Lerner Publications Company
A division of Lerner Publishing Group, Inc.
241 First Avenue North
Minneapolis, MN 55401 USA

For reading levels and more information, look
up this title at www.lernerbooks.com.

Main body text set in ITC Franklin Gothic Std
Book Condensed 12/15.
Typeface provided by Adobe Systems.

Library of Congress Cataloging-in-Publication
Data

Bailer, Darice.
       What's great about Vermont? / Darice
Bailer.
           pages cm
       Includes index.
       Audience: Grades 4–6.
       ISBN 978-1-4677-3876-7 (lb : alk.
paper) — ISBN 978-1-4677-8517-4 (pb :
alk. paper) — ISBN 978-1-4677-8518-1
(eb pdf)
       1. Vermont—Juvenile literature. I. Title.
F49.3.B28 2015
974.3—dc23   2015000983

Manufactured in the United States of America
1 – PC – 7/15/15

LAKE CHAMPLAIN MARITIME MUSEUM ✳ 16

ECHO LAKE AQUARIUM AND SCIENCE CENTER ✳ 18

SAM MAZZA'S FARM MARKET ✳ 20

OKEMO MOUNTAIN RESORT ✳ 22

BEN & JERRY'S WATERBURY FACTORY ✳ 24

VERMONT BY MAP ✳ 26
VERMONT FACTS ✳ 28
GLOSSARY ✳ 30
FURTHER INFORMATION ✳ 31
INDEX ✳ 32

VERMONT Welcomes You!

Do you like hiking up mountains? What about tubing down snow-covered hills? Known for the mountains that run through it, the Green Mountain State is one of the most beautiful states in the country. Vermont's mountains and lakes are fun all year round! Hike past the brightly colored leaves in fall. Then go dashing through the snow on a dogsled in winter. People also come to Vermont for its tasty foods: cheese, chocolate, ice cream, and maple syrup. Visit to see for yourself how all are made. But first, turn the page to read about ten things that make Vermont great!

Welcome To

VERMONT

THE GREEN MOUNTAIN STATE

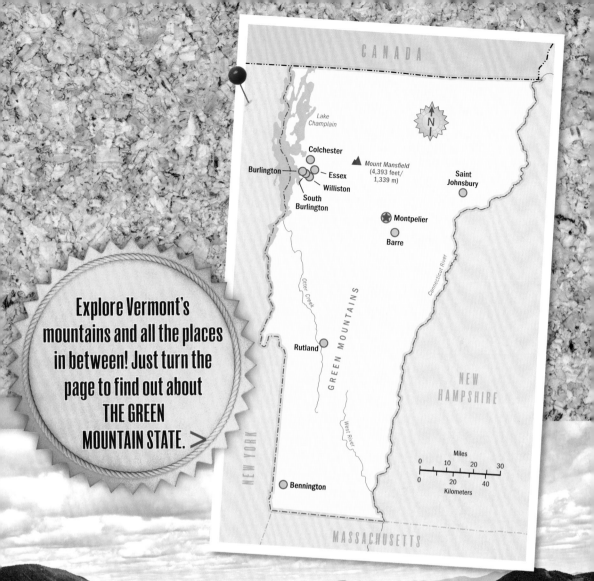

Explore Vermont's mountains and all the places in between! Just turn the page to find out about THE GREEN MOUNTAIN STATE.

CANADA

Lake
Champlain

Colchester

Burlington

Essex

Williston

South
Burlington

▲ Mount Mansfield
(4,393 feet/
1,339 m)

Saint
Johnsbury

★ Montpelier

Barre

Otter Creek

GREEN MOUNTAINS

Connecticut River

Rutland

West River

NEW
HAMPSHIRE

NEW YORK

Bennington

Miles
0   10   20   30
0   20   40
Kilometers

MASSACHUSETTS

Child performers amaze the crowds at Circus Smirkus shows.

CIRCUS SMIRKUS

> Grab a parent and run away to the circus! Circus Smirkus in Greensboro is not like other circuses. All Circus Smirkus stars are ten- to eighteen-year-olds. The Smirkus Big Top Tour performs dozens of shows in Vermont during the summer. Girls and boys dress up like clowns with red noses and painted cheeks. Count the number of balls a juggler tosses into the air. And don't miss the high-wire act. Could you stand on a thin wire suspended 6 feet (1.8 meters) off the ground, leap up, and land without falling? Watch as performers swing overhead on trapezes. Some circus teens ride unicycles taller than they are!

When the show is over, you'll have the chance to meet the stars and ask for their autographs. Did you know you can join the circus? Sign up for Circus Smirkus Camp. What acts would you like to perform? Learn fun tricks and take your own place in the ring!

Watch acrobats suspended from silk perform tricks at a Circus Smirkus show.

BRATTLEBORO

> Retreat Farm in Brattleboro invites you to pet cows, lambs, chicks, and many other animals! The farm is open from Memorial Day weekend until October each year. You can see a baby chick hatch from an egg, and you can play with lambs. Next, get ready to work! There is a lot to be done on the farm. Help brush a miniature horse, or feed a little goat from a bottle. Pour some animal food into a bowl for an emu to peck.

While in Brattleboro, visit the Creamery Covered Bridge. There used to be many covered bridges in Brattleboro, but now only the Creamery Bridge remains. Walk across on a built-in sidewalk. Then be sure to stop next door at the Grafton Village Cheese. Here you can watch cheddar cheese being made. Then try a piece! Grafton makes its cheese with milk from small Vermont farms. Enjoy a picnic with cheese and crackers from Grafton. The outdoor tables offer great views of Vermont's beautiful mountains.

Hold a newborn chick at the Retreat Farm.

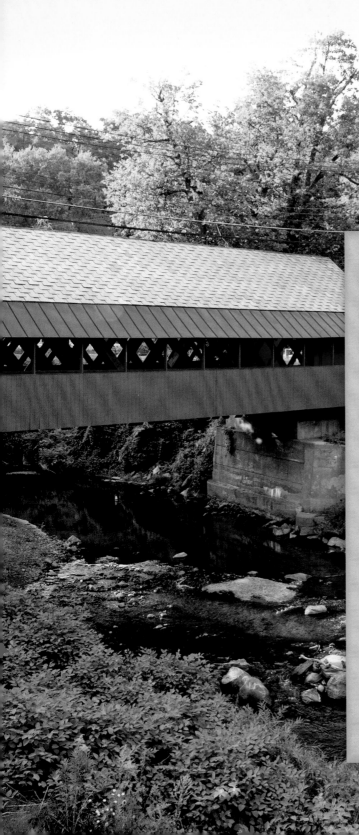

VERMONT DAIRY FARMS

Dairy farming is an important industry in Vermont. In the 1600s, settlers arrived from Europe. They brought cows with them to feed their families. In the late 1800s, selling dairy products became easier with the arrival of railroads. In 2012, there were 995 dairy farms in Vermont. Each Vermont dairy farm has an average of 130 cows. Vermont cows produced more than 302 million gallons (1.1 billion liters) of milk in 2013. That would be more than one gallon for every person living in the United States!

REVOLUTIONARY WAR SITES

> Visit some of the most historic spots in Vermont. First, ride an elevator to the top of Bennington Battle Monument in Bennington. It is more than 306 feet (93 m) tall! This monument was built after the Revolutionary War (1775-1783). During the war, American colonists defended food and weapons where the monument now sits. Bennington Monument is the tallest building in Vermont. From the observation deck at the top, you can see three states! View the hills and valleys of Vermont, Massachusetts, and New York.

Make your next stop the Mount Independence State Historic Site in Orwell. Here, you can pretend you're a war detective. Your job is to figure out what happened at Mount Independence. Historians know the answer. But you get to solve the mystery for yourself. Begin with the talking sculpture of American and British soldiers. Then ask at the front desk for a copy of the *History Detectives Scavenger Hunt*. Write down your answers with a quill pen. Good luck solving the mystery!

REVOLUTIONARY WAR

Great Britain wanted American colonists to obey the British government and pay taxes. The colonists thought some of the taxes were unfair. They also wanted more freedom to govern themselves. The conflict led to the Revolutionary War. The American colonists defeated the British and won their independence from Great Britain.

Catch the tristate view from the top of the Bennington Battle Monument.

VERMONT MAPLE FESTIVAL

> Do you like maple syrup on your pancakes and waffles? Vermont makes more maple syrup than any other state. Check out Saint Albans, where the Vermont Maple Festival takes place each spring. Maple sugar season starts when snow begins to melt and winter ends. Then, when the work of making the syrup is just about finished, the celebration starts. Marching bands and classic cars parade down Saint Albans's Main Street. Ride a pony or whirl on a carnival ride. Watch a clown twist balloons into animal shapes. There are activities for kids all weekend long. A kids' talent show, a puppet show, and a dog show offer endless options for entertainment.

Have you ever wondered how sap from a sugar maple tree is made into maple syrup? Ride a bus to a sugarhouse and find out! You'll see how sap flows out of a sugar maple. Don't miss tasting a maple sugar candy shaped like a leaf. Yum!

MAPLE SYRUP

Maple syrup comes from the sap of maple trees. The sap is tapped from the trees in the spring. Workers drill small holes in the trees. Then they stick a metal spout in the hole, which allows the sap to drain into buckets. Or they might run tubes from a tree all the way to a sugarhouse. That's a building where workers boil the sap. As the sap boils, water evaporates and only pure maple syrup remains. That syrup is bottled and shipped to stores. Vermont bottled 1.3 million gallons (4.9 million liters) of maple syrup in 2013. That's enough syrup to pour on millions of pancakes and waffles around the world!

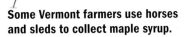

Some Vermont farmers use horses
and sleds to collect maple syrup.

BILLINGS FARM & MUSEUM

> Have you ever watched cows being milked or chickens laying eggs? You can see both at the Billings Farm & Museum in Woodstock. Hear sheep bleat and horses neigh all year round! Start your visit by exploring the old 1890 farmhouse. You can help make homemade butter. Turn the crank of a churn to make butter the old-fashioned way. In June, the museum holds Ice Cream Sundays. You can also help make the ice cream! If you visit on the third Sunday in July, you'll be there for National Ice Cream Day. Will you pick chocolate, vanilla, strawberry, or blueberry?

Out at the barn, meet the farm's horses, sheep, and calves. In May, you can see a Border collie dog herd sheep. And you won't want to miss visiting Billings Farm & Museum for its Family Halloween event in the fall. Dress up in a costume and march in a Halloween parade. Carve a pumpkin and hear a Halloween tale. Care to try pumpkin bowling? Pick up a round pumpkin and use it to knock down plastic milk cartons. Then climb on a wagon for a horse-drawn ride around the fields. If you come back in winter, take a horse-drawn sleigh ride through the snow!

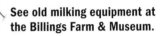
See old milking equipment at the Billings Farm & Museum.

Would you like to pet one of the farm's cows?

LAKE CHAMPLAIN MARITIME MUSEUM

Try on an old diving helmet at the Lake Champlain Maritime Museum.

> Ahoy, matey! There are more than three hundred shipwrecks at the bottom of Vermont's Lake Champlain. Learn all about them and see some for yourself at the Lake Champlain Maritime Museum in Vergennes. The *Philadelphia* sank in 1776, but you can still see what it looked like. The museum has a replica that you can climb aboard.

Then head outside and take a boat ride on the lake to see the remains of *Champlain II*. A small yellow and black machine plunges off your boat and into the water. The machine's name is Bob, and it has a camera. Bob finds the wreck and flashes pictures on a screen you can see on the boat. These pictures show *Champlain II*, which sank more than one hundred years ago!

Back inside the museum, see a special submarine built to explore the lake. And don't miss the Kids Pirate Festival in June. Come dressed as a pirate. Learn about a pirate's life at sea and get a temporary pirate tattoo. Make and decorate your own cardboard treasure chest. Yo, ho, ho!

VERMONT NAMES

Vermont's name is a combination of the French words *ver* and *mont*. *Ver* is from *vert*, the French word for "green." *Mont* is from the word *montagne*, or "mountain." The two words mean "green mountain or hill," which Vermont has many of. Lake Champlain is named after a French explorer, Samuel de Champlain (*above*). In 1609, he visited the area and named the lake after himself.

ECHO LAKE
AQUARIUM AND SCIENCE CENTER

> The Abenaki and Iroquois American Indians of Vermont often told of a strange creature in Lake Champlain. The monster became known as Champ after French explorer Samuel de Champlain claimed he saw it in 1609. But is the monster real? Go to ECHO Lake Aquarium and Science Center in Burlington and decide for yourself! Watch a film in which scientists tell you what they think. Check out a color photo taken in 1977. Do you think that's Champ's head poking out of the lake?

In early spring, snow melts and turns to muck on Vermont's dirt roads. People in Vermont call this mud season. ECHO celebrates by holding an Earth Weeks' MudFest for sixteen days in spring! Dig your hands into the mud! The museum hosts a Mud Fling that's not to be missed. Climb to a third-floor balcony that overlooks the lake. The museum sets up a giant target for you below. It's a tarp with a painted bull's-eye. Fire a mud ball at the target!

Do you believe Champ the lake creature exists in Lake Champlain?

CHAZY FOSSIL REEF

Approximately half a billion years ago, an ancient sea covered Vermont. A reef from that ocean still exists in Lake Champlain. Chazy Fossil Reef is found on Isle La Motte. The reef is 480 million years old. That makes it the world's oldest reef. Strange animals lived here millions of years ago, creating fossils. One was an ancestor of the modern squid.

SAM MAZZA'S FARM MARKET

> Vermont is a-MAZE-ing in the fall! Leaves turn as bright as red, yellow, and orange crayons. Pumpkins ripen in the pumpkin patches. Start your fall fun at Sam Mazza's Farm Market in Colchester. The farm holds a Giant Pumpkin Weigh-In each September. Have you ever seen a pumpkin that weighs more than 1,000 pounds (454 kilograms)?

Check out the farm's two corn mazes. They each have mystery games for you to solve. In one, Farmer Joe is missing. Pretend you're a farm detective. Clues are waiting for you at checkpoints within the maze. Can you figure out what happened to Farmer Joe?

Before leaving, take the hayride out to the pumpkin patch. Once you arrive, find the perfect pumpkin to take home and carve.

Choose your favorite pumpkin at Sam Mazza's Farm Market.

See enormous pumpkins at the Giant Pumpkin Weigh-In.

OKEMO MOUNTAIN RESORT

> Vermont's ski resorts are famous. Okemo Mountain Resort in Ludlow is a blast during summer or winter! Zip down the mountain on the Timber Ripper Mountain Coaster all year round. This roller coaster starts with a five-minute climb up Okemo Mountain. Go fast or slow down the track, past the trees, and along the twists and turns. You control your speed, and you can fly up to 25 miles (40 kilometers) per hour! Then jump on a trampoline while attached to a bungee cord. Test your courage on a tree challenge course. Can you hold onto a rope and swing from one wooden platform to another? Don't look down! Next, try the zip line. Leap off a wooden starting perch, and fly through the air on a harness!

In winter, it's snow time! Fly down the hill and up a snowy ramp on a snowboard or skis. Soar into the air. Land on a soft green air bag after catching some air! Do you like tubing? There's the Snowtubing Park where you can ride with a friend. Not far away are some Siberian huskies who love to run! They'll take you dogsledding at Braeburn Siberians in Windsor. Kneel down and give the dogs a hug before your forty-five-minute ride. Then sit down in one of the sleds. Whoosh through the woods on a snowy trail.

Test your snowboarding skills on Okemo Mountain!

Pick up your own pair of skis at the Okemo ski swap.

BEN & JERRY'S
WATERBURY FACTORY

Snack on your favorite ice cream flavor at the Ben & Jerry's Waterbury Factory.

> Who doesn't love ice cream? You can see how ice cream is made at the Ben & Jerry's Waterbury Factory in Waterbury. Ben Cohen and Jerry Greenfield started the ice cream company in 1978. In Waterbury, watch a movie and get the scoop on the company's history. Then go on a thirty-minute guided tour of the factory. Watch the ice cream churn in the workroom. See some of the delicious flavors being made. And yes, you can have a free taste! It might be a new flavor that the company made up. Or you could try chocolate chip cookie dough. It's the most popular Ben & Jerry's flavor. If you and your family are really hungry at the end of your tour, order the Vermonster! It's a monster of an ice cream sundae. What's in it? Twenty scoops of ice cream, four bananas, brownies, cookies, M&M'S, Reese's Pieces, chocolate sprinkles, hot fudge, and caramel. And it's smothered in whipped cream!

See a display of the different Ben & Jerry's ice cream flavors.

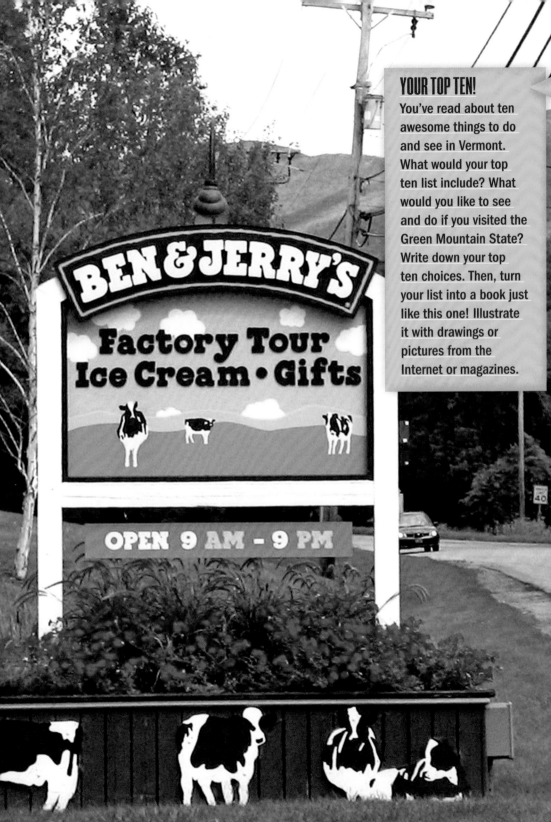

YOUR TOP TEN!
You've read about ten awesome things to do and see in Vermont. What would your top ten list include? What would you like to see and do if you visited the Green Mountain State? Write down your top ten choices. Then, turn your list into a book just like this one! Illustrate it with drawings or pictures from the Internet or magazines.

> MAP KEY

⭐ Capital city

◯ City

◯ Point of interest

▲ Highest elevation

—··— International border

—·— State border

Visit www.lerneresource.com to learn more about the state flag of Vermont.

CANADA

Lake Champlain

● **Vermont Maple Festival**
(Saint Albans)

ECHO Lake Aquarium and Science Center

Sam Mazza's Farm Market

● **Circus Smirkus**
(Greensboro)

Colchester

▲ Mount Mansfield
(4,393 feet/
1,339 m)

Burlington

Essex

● Saint
Johnsbury

Williston

Ben & Jerry's Waterbury Factory
(Waterbury)

South
Burlington

★ Montpelier

● **Lake Champlain Maritime Museum**
(Vergennes)

● Barre

Connecticut River

Otter Creek

G R E E N   M O U N T A I N S

● **Billings Farm & Museum**
(Woodstock)

Rutland

● **Okemo Mountain Resort**
(Ludlow)

NEW
YORK

NEW
HAMPSHIRE

West River

Bennington Battle Monument

Bennington

● **Retreat Farm**
(Brattleboro)

Miles
0   10   20   30
0   20   40
Kilometers

MASSACHUSETTS

VERMONT FACTS

NICKNAME: The Green Mountain State

SONG: "These Green Mountains" by Diane Martin and Rita Buglass Gluck

MOTTO: "Freedom and Unity"

> **FLOWER:** red clover

TREE: sugar maple

> **BIRD:** hermit thrush

ANIMAL: Morgan horse

> **BEVERAGE:** milk

DATE AND RANK OF STATEHOOD: March 4, 1791; the 14th state

> **CAPITAL:** Montpelier

AREA: 9,615 square miles (24,903 sq. km)

AVERAGE JANUARY TEMPERATURE: 19°F (−7°C)

AVERAGE JULY TEMPERATURE: 69°F (21°C)

POPULATION AND RANK: 626,630; 50th (2013)

MAJOR CITIES AND POPULATIONS: Burlington (42,284), South Burlington (18,612), Rutland (16,126), Barre (8,927), Montpelier (7,755)

NUMBER OF US CONGRESS MEMBERS: 1 representative, 2 senators

NUMBER OF ELECTORAL VOTES: 3

NATURAL RESOURCES: granite, marble, slate, talc, trees

AGRICULTURAL PRODUCTS: apples, cheese, chickens, ice cream, maple syrup, sheep, sweet corn

MANUFACTURED GOODS: electronics, food products, furniture, machinery

STATE HOLIDAYS AND CELEBRATIONS: Bennington Battle Day, Vermont Maple Festival

GLOSSARY

churn: a container in which cream is stirred or shaken to make butter

colonist: a person who has left his or her country to settle in a new area

emu: a large bird from Australia that runs fast but doesn't fly

sap: the liquid that carries food and water through a tree or other plant

trapeze: a short bar hung high above the ground by two ropes. Circus performers hold the bar and perform tricks.

unicycle: a vehicle or bike with one wheel and no handlebars

LERNER

SOURCE

Expand learning beyond the printed book. Download free, complementary educational resources for this book from our website, www.lerneresource.com.

FURTHER INFORMATION

Amstel, Marsha. *The Horse-Riding Adventure of Sybil Ludington, Revolutionary War Messenger*. Adapted by Amanda Doering Tourville. Minneapolis: Graphic Universe, 2012. Read about Sybil Ludington's risky ride to warn of the British Army's arrival during the Revolutionary War.

Friesen, Helen Lepp. *Vermont: The Green Mountain State*. New York: AV2 by Weigl, 2012. Learn more about the history and the state symbols of Vermont.

Schnobrich, Emily. *Vermont: The Green Mountain State*. Minneapolis: Bellwether Media, 2014. Read more about the geography and the culture of Vermont.

Vermont History, Facts & Fun
https://www.sec.state.vt.us/kids/pubs/history_facts_fun.pdf
Learn cool facts about the Green Mountain State.

Vermont History Trek
http://www.vermontvacation.com/VermontHistoryTrek.aspx
Find out about all the adventures, scavenger hunts, and treasure hunts waiting for you in Vermont. Print the activity guide. Make a journal. Win a prize!

Vermont Secretary of State: Kids Pages
https://www.sec.state.vt.us/kids/index.html
Read more about the great state of Vermont and listen to Vermont's state song!

INDEX

Ben & Jerry's Waterbury Factory, 24

Bennington Battle Monument, 10

Billings Farm & Museum, 14

Brattleboro, 8

Champlain, Samuel de, 17, 18

Champlain II, 16

Chazy Fossil Reef, 19

Circus Smirkus, 6

Colchester, 20

Creamery Covered Bridge, 8

dairy farms, 9

Earth Weeks' MudFest, 18

ECHO Lake Aquarium and Science Center, 18

Grafton Village Cheese, 8

Greensboro, 6

Lake Champlain, 16, 17, 18, 19

Lake Champlain Maritime Museum, 16

Ludlow, 22

maple syrup, 4, 12

maps, 5, 26–27

Mount Independence State Historic Site, 10

Okemo Mountain Resort, 22

Philadelphia, 16

Retreat Farm, 8

Revolutionary War, 10, 11

Saint Albans, 12

Sam Mazza's Farm Market, 20

Vermont Maple Festival, 12

Waterbury, 24

PHOTO ACKNOWLEDGMENTS

The images in this book are used with the permission of: © Don Land/Shutterstock Images, p. 1; NASA, pp. 2–3; © Laura Westlund/Independent Picture Service, pp. 5 (top), 27; © wellesenterprises/iStockphoto, p. 4; © Jay Boucher/Shutterstock Images, p. 5 (bottom); © hbp pix CC 2.0, pp. 6–7, 6 (bottom); © Toby Talbot/AP Images, pp. 6 (top), 16–17, 23 (bottom), 24 (top); © Liquid Productions, LLC/Shutterstock Images, pp. 8–9; © Warren Goldswain/Shutterstock Images, p. 8; © branislavpudar/Shutterstock Images, p. 9; © Ed Young/Corbis, pp. 10–11; © Bosc d'Anjou CC 2.0, p. 11 (bottom); Domenick D'Andrea, p. 11 (top); © Prisma Bildagentur AG/Alamy, pp. 12–13; © Kevin Fleming/Corbis, p. 13; © Joe Mercier/Shutterstock Images, p. 12; © Reimar 5/Alamy, pp. 14–15; © Brad Mitchell/Alamy, p. 15 (top); © Phil Schermeister/Corbis, p. 15 (bottom); © Daniel Borzynski/Alamy, p. 16; Library of Congress, p. 17 (LC-USZ62-33292); Mfwills, pp. 18–19; © Macduff Everton/RGB Ventures/Alamy, p. 19; © Jerry Hopman/iStockphoto, p. 18; © Geraldass/iStockphoto, pp. 20–21; © Digital Vision/Photodisc/Thinkstock, p. 21 (left); © Michael Gaffney/iStock/Thinkstock, p. 21 (right); © Adam Ford/iStock/Thinkstock, pp. 22–23; © Frankysze/iStockphoto, p. 23 (top); SNSAnchor, pp. 24–25; © Kris Tripplaar/Sipa USA/Newscom, p. 24 (bottom); © Atlaspix/Shutterstock Images, p. 26; © Mickael Buono/Shutterstock Images, p. 29 (top); © Stubblefield Photography/Shutterstock Images, p. 29 (middle left); © Chursina Viktoriia/Shutterstock Images, p. 29 (middle right); © Jeffrey M. Frank/Shutterstock Images, p. 29 (bottom).

Cover: © iStockphoto.com/pokergecko (maple syrup); courtesy of the Vermont Giant Pumpkin Growers, photo by Daniel Boyce (pumpkin boat); © Anton Oparin/Dreamstime.com (skier); © Darren McCollester/Getty Images (Circus Smirkus); © Laura Westlund/Independent Picture Service (map); © iStockphoto.com/fpm (seal); © iStockphoto.com/vicm (pushpins); © iStockphoto.com/benz190 (corkboard).